French - Bulgarian

LEARNING FLASHCARDS

FOR BABIES TODDLERS

alligator

алигатор

The alligator is having a party.

fourmi

мравка

The ant is red.

ours

мечка

The bear loves you.

abeille

пчела

The bee is saying hello.

oiseau

птица

The bird is flying.

papillon

пеперуда

The butterfly is pretty.

chameau

камила

The camel has a hump.

chat

котка

The cat is happy.

dinosaure

динозавър

The dinosaur is laying eggs.

poulet

пиле

The chicken is dancing.

vache

крава

The cow has a bell.

cerf

елен

The reindeer has a toy.

chien

куче

The dog has two floppy ears.

dauphin

делфин

The dolphin is swimming.

canard

патица

The duck has a bow.

aigle

орел

The eagle is looking for food.

l'éléphant

слон

The elephant is sitting.

poisson

риба

The fish is a clownfish.

libellule

водно конче

The dragonfly is blue.

renard

лисица

The fox has a red nose.

grenouille

жаба

The frog is smiling.

girafe

жираф

The giraffe has a long neck.

chèvre

коза

The goat has a beard

ver de terre

червей

The worm is in the apple

poule

кокошка

The hen has chicks.

hippopotame

хипопотам

The hippo is big.

cheval

кон

The horse is fast.

kangourou

кенгуру

The kangaroo has a baby.

chaton

коте

The kitten is playing.

lion

лъв

The lion has a mane.

homard

омар

The lobster is red.

singe

маймуна

The monkey has a tail.

poulpe

октопод

The octopus has food.

hibou

бухал

The owls have big eyes.

panda

панда

The panda wears a diaper.

porc

прасе

The pig is fat and pink.

chiot

кученце

The dog is brown.

lapin

заек

The rabbit has a carrot.

rat

плъх

The mouse is writing something.

crabe

рак

The crab has two pinchers.

requin

акула

The shark is scary.

mouton

овца

The sheep are very fluffy.

escargot

охлюв

The snail is slow.

serpent

змия

The snake has poison.

araignée

паяк

The spider is purple.

écureuil

катерица

The squirrel has a nut.

tigre

тигър

The tiger has a red bow.

tortue

костенурка

The turtle has a shell.

loup

вълк

The wolf is smiling.

zèbre

зебра

The zebra is black and white.

dinde

турция

The turkey has two legs.

coq

петел

The rooster will crow.

perroquet

папагал

The parrot is colorful.

hérisson

таралеж

The hedgehog has apples.

pomme

ябълка

The apple has a leaf.

abricot

кайсия

The apricot is yellow.

avocat

авокадо

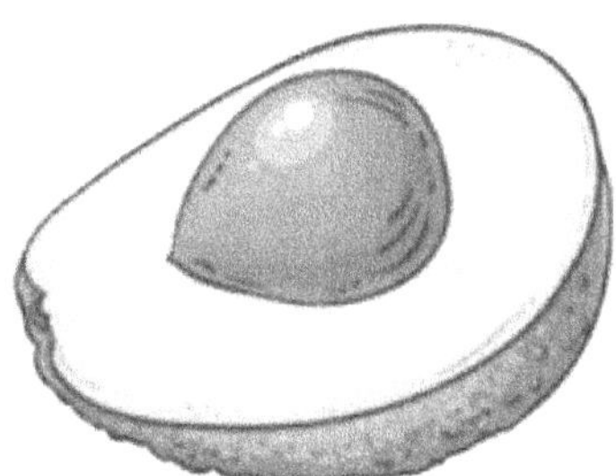

The avocado has a nut.

banane

банан

The banana is yellow.

la mûre

къпина

There are a lot of blackberries.

cassis

касис

The blackcurrants are yummy.

myrtille

боровинка

The blueberries are sweet.

cerise

череша

The cherries have a stem.

noix de coco

кокосов орех

The coconuts have juice.

figues

смокини

The fig has seeds.

grain de raisin

гроздов

The grapes are purple.

pamplemousse

грейпфрут

The grapefruits are sour.

kiwi

киви

The kiwi is fresh.

citron

лимон

The lemons are yellow.

citron vert

вар

We have lots of lime.

litchi

личи

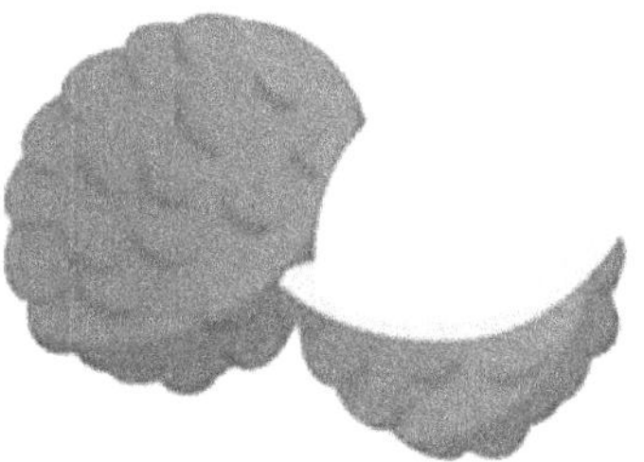

I like to eat lychee.

mandarine

мандарин портокал

Oranges are refreshing.

mangue

манго

Mango is my favorite fruit.

orange

оранжев

Mandarins are like oranges.

papaye

папая

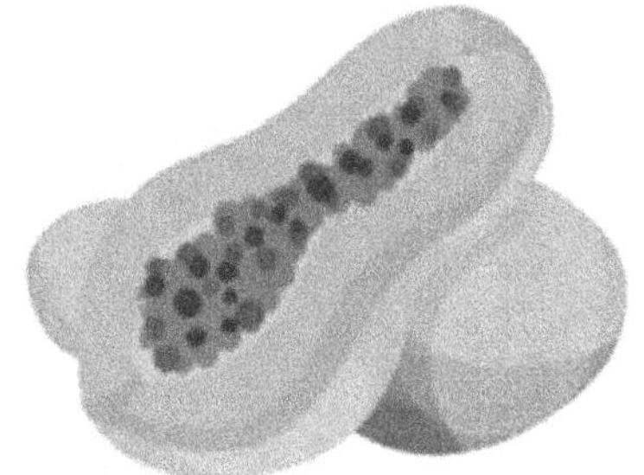

Papayas have lots of seeds.

pêche

праскова

Peaches are juicy.

poire

круша

Pears have a strange figure.

ananas

ананас

The pineapple has a thumbs up.

prune

слива

Plums are healthy for you.

grenade

нар

Pomegranates are all red.

framboise

малина

The raspberry is shiny.

fraise

ягода

The strawberry has leaves on top.

pastèque

диня

The watermelon is big.

mandarine

мандарина

The tangerine looks like an orange.

tarte

пай

I like to eat apple pie.

gâteau

торта

That cake is huge.

bonbons

бонбони

Candy is not good for your teeth.

biscuit

курабийка

Cookies are easy to make.

donut

поничка

I like strawberry donuts.

crème glacée

сладолед

The ice cream is melting.

muffin

кифла

The muffin has a cute wrapper.

pudding

пудинг

We eat pudding on Christmas.

classeur

папка

I keep pictures in my binder.

livre

книга

I like to eat books.

sac à dos

раница

The backpack has lots of stuff.

les ciseaux

ножици

I have scissors in my bag.

épingles

pins

Pins can hold stuff up.

agrafe

клипс

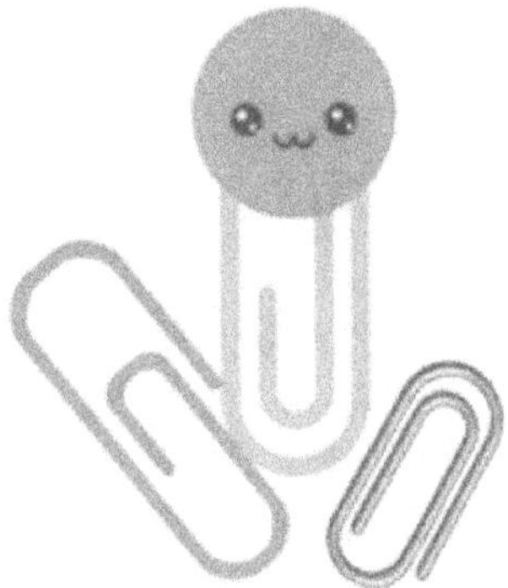

Clips can hold up paper.

papier

хартия

I have lots of paper.

agrafeuse

телбод

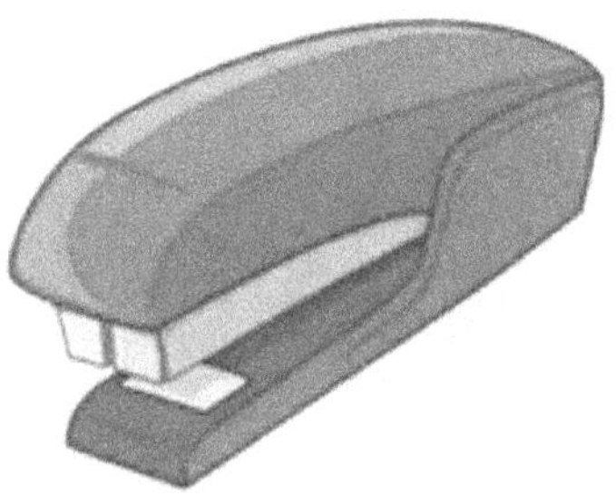

My stapler is shiny and red.

calculatrice

калкулатор

My calculator has buttons.

règle

владетел

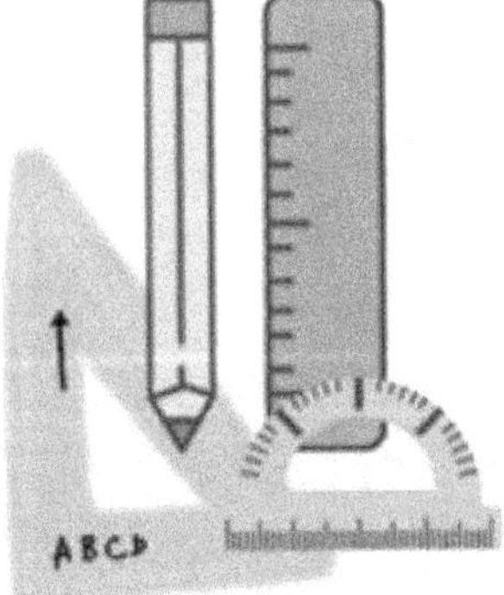

I have lots of rulers.

la colle

лепило

The glue is sticky.

bibliothèque

библиотечка

My bookcase has lots of things.

calendrier

календар

I have a calendar on my table.

chaise

председател

My chair is fancy.

l'horloge

часовник

The clock says that it's 3 o'clock.

ordinateur

компютър

I do things on my computer.

bureaux

бюра

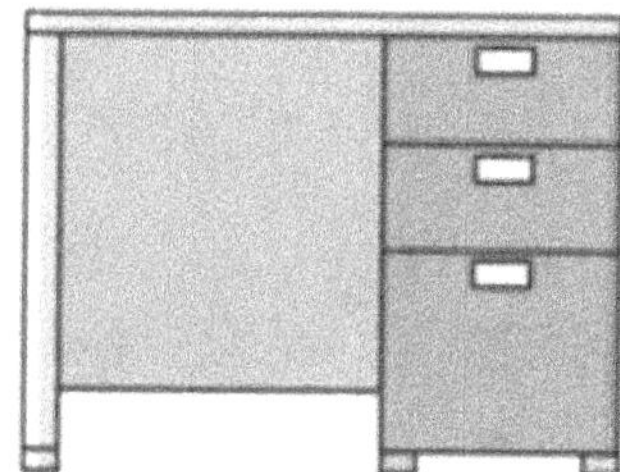

I put lots of things on my desk.

dictionnaire

речник

The dictionary has lots of words.

la gomme

гума

Erasers are used with pencils.

carte

карта

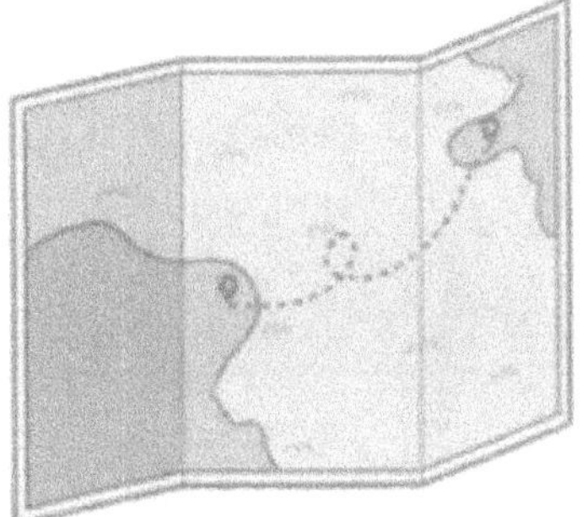

The map shows you different places.

carnet

тетрадка

I use notebooks at school.

stylo

химилка

My pen is very pretty.

crayon

молив

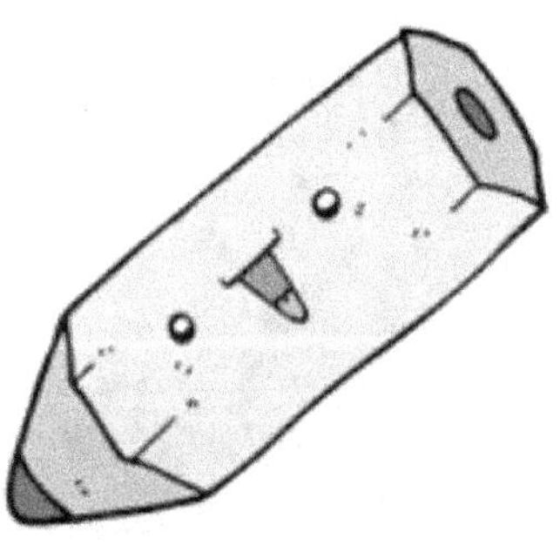

My friend gave me a pencil.

ceinture

колан

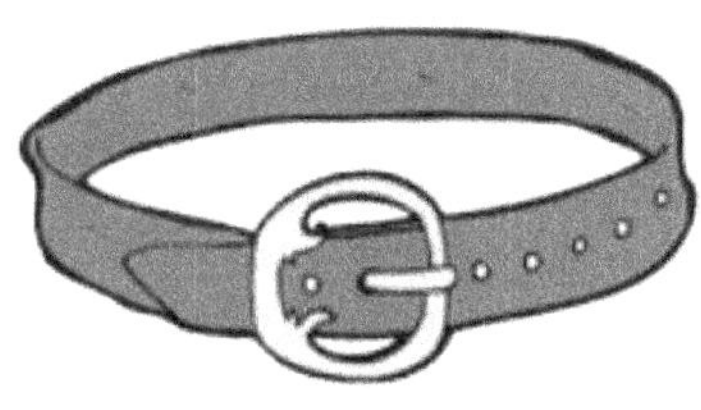

I have a belt on my pants.

bottes

ботуши

I have big brown boots.

chapeau

шапка

My mom bought me a new cap.

manteau

палто

She has a long yellow coat.

robes

облича се

My dress has a bow.

gants

ръкавици

I got new gloves.

chapeau

шапка

That hat is for a wicked witch.

veste

яке

The jacket is cozy.

jeans

дънки

My jeans are long.

pyjamas

пижама

I sleep in my pajamas.

un pantalon

панталони

The bear is wearing pants.

imperméable

дъждобран

We wear our raincoats when it is raining.

écharpe

шал

The baby has a scarf around his neck.

chemise

риза

I like this shirt the best.

des chaussures

обувки

I have red and blue shoes.

jupe

пола

My skirt has lots of buttons.

pantalon

спортни панталони

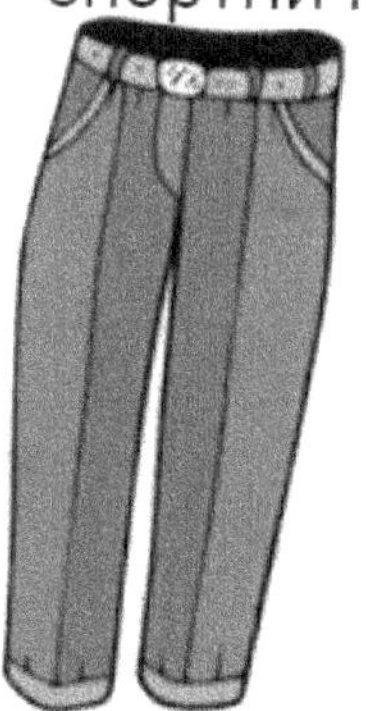

My dad wears slacks.

chaussons

домашни пантофи

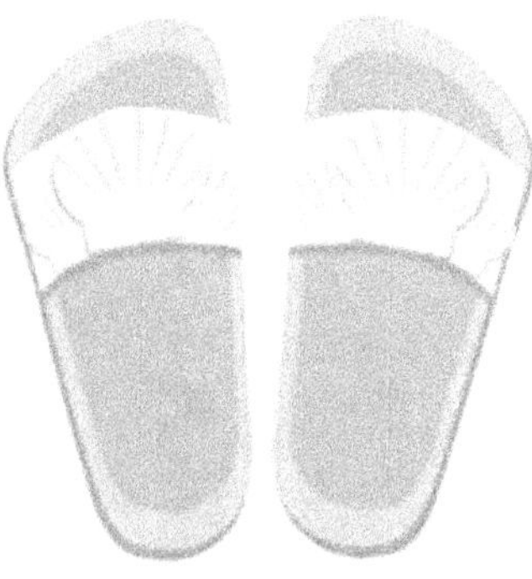

I have seashells on my sandals.

chaussettes

чорапи

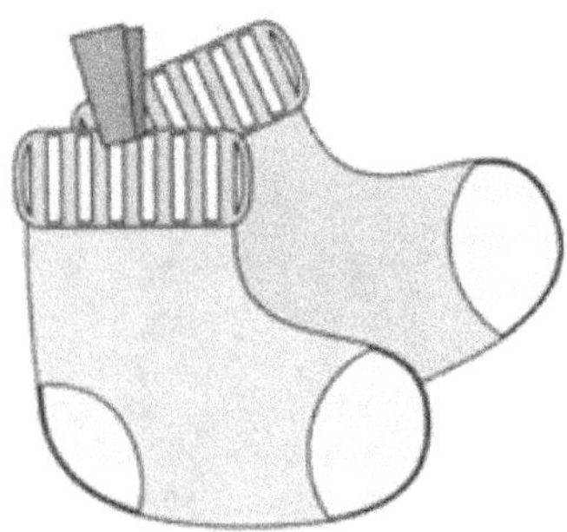

My baby sister wears socks.

costume

костюм

My brother is wearing a suit.

chandail

пуловер

I am wearing a sweater for winter.

cravate

вратовръзка

My dad wears a tie to meetings.

pantalon

панталони

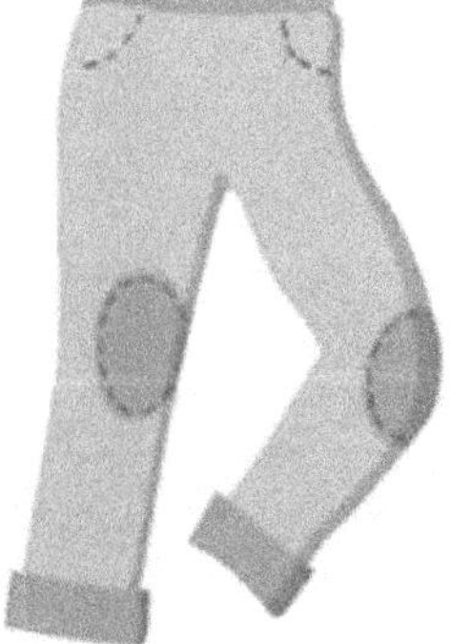

The trousers look like jeans.

slip

долни гащи

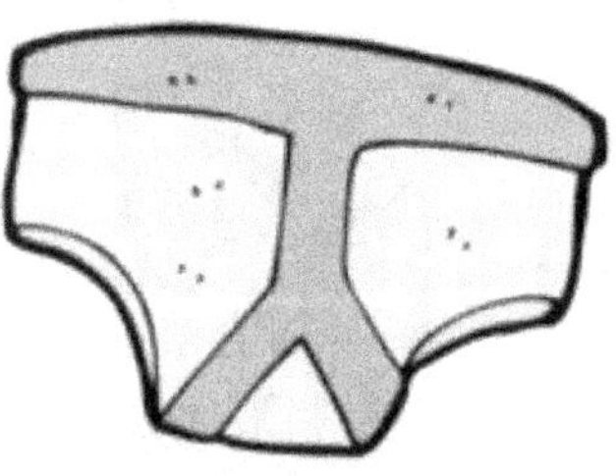

I always wear my underwear.

maillot de corps

долна

My undershirt has a star.

une

един

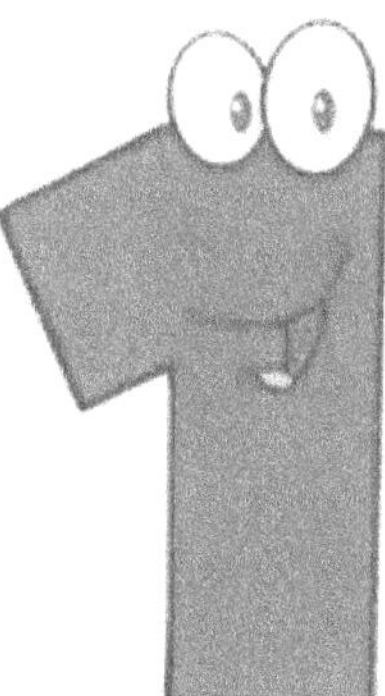

Number one and the bee are friends.

deux

две

The cat and the mouse both love two.

trois

три

The bear gives number three a present.

quatre

четири

Number four is a home for the cat.

cinq

пет

Number five hatches an egg.

six

шест

Number six is going to eat a carrot.

sept

седем

Number seven is playing with the tiger.

huit

осем

Number eight is funny.

neuf

девет

Number nine meets the parrot.

dix

десет

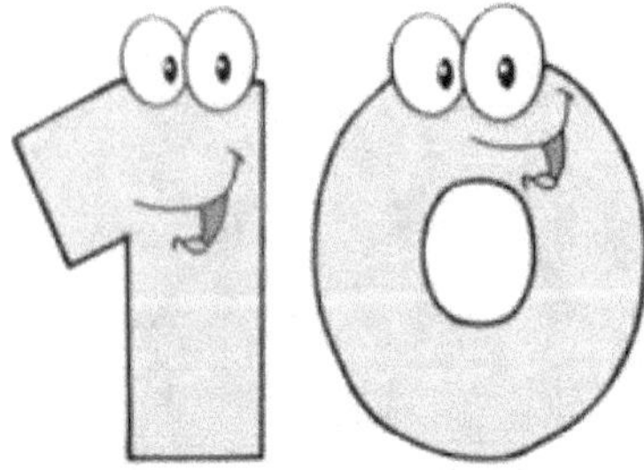

Number ten is smiling.

onze

единадесет

Number eleven has big eyes.

douze

дванадесет

Number twelve is number one and two.

treize

тринадесет

Number thirteen is excited.

quatorze

четиринадесет

The number fourteen is vast.

quinze

петнадесет

The number fifteen is green.

seize

шестнадесет

Sixteen is my lucky number.

dix-sept

седемнадесет

Number seventeen look alike.

dix-huit

осемнадесет

Number eighteen will go to the circus.

dix-neuf

деветнадесет

I am nineteen now!

vingt

двадесет

Number twenty has a zero.

fourmi

мравка

The ant has lots of legs.

cloche

звънец

The bell will ring.

vache

крава

The cow has a bow.

poupée

кукла

She has a cute bear doll.

oeuf

яйце

The chick has hatched out of the egg.

poisson

риба

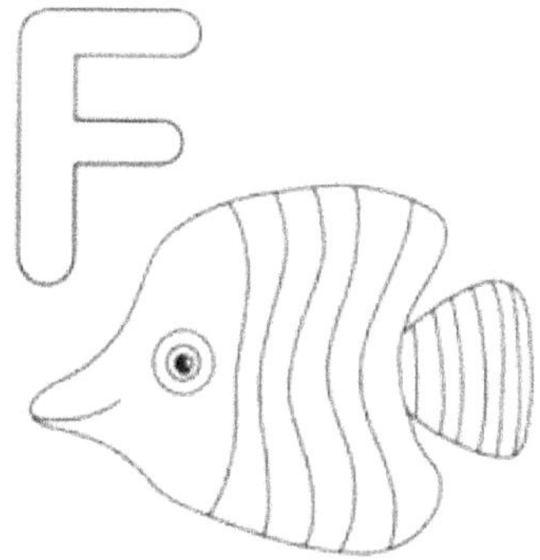

The fish is swimming in the water.

chèvre

коза

The goat is sitting on the grass.

chapeau

шапка

He is wearing a hat.

crème glacée

сладолед

I like to eat ice cream.

confiture

конфитюр

The kitten is sitting on the jam jar.

chaton

коте

The cat is sleeping on the floor.

lion

лъв

The lion is waiting for the tiger.

rat

плъх

The mouse has lots of presents.

nez

нос

The reindeer has a red nose.

hibou

бухал

The owl is sleeping.

porc

прасе

P

The pig will eat cupcakes.

reine

кралица

Q

The queen has a big crown.

lapin

заек

R

The rabbit is jumping up and down.

mouton

овца

S

The sheep have fluffy wool.

tortue

костенурка

T

The turtle has a shell.

parapluie

чадър

U

The mouse is holding an umbrella.

van

фургон

The van is driving along the road.

pastèque

диня

The watermelon has lots of seeds.

xylophone

ксилофон

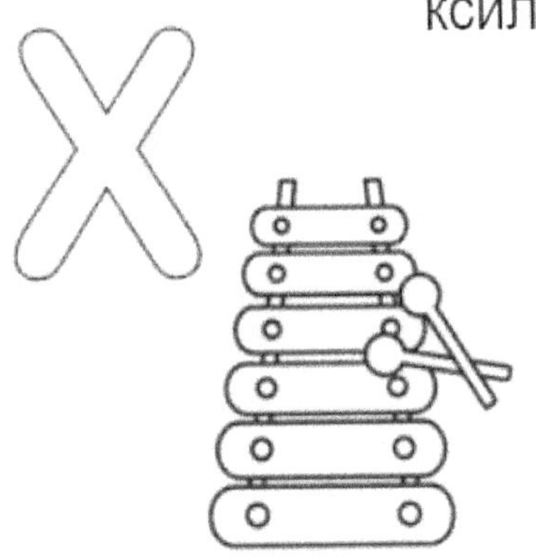

We are going to play the xylophone.

yaourt

кисело мляко

We opened the yogurt can.

zèbre

зебра

The zebra is surprised.

rose

розов

Most of my clothes are pink.

marron

кафяв

color the word and
the picture in pink

brown

My chocolate is brown.

gris

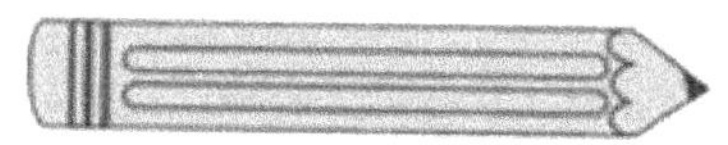

сив

color the word and
the picture in pink

gray

I don't like the color gray.

vert

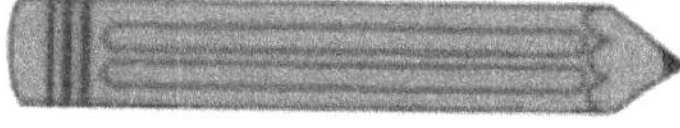

зелен

color the word and
the picture in pink

green

The vegetables are green.

jaune

жълт

color the word and
the picture in pink

yellow

Bananas are yellow.

blanc

бял

color the word and
the picture in pink

white

The paper that I write on is white.

rouge

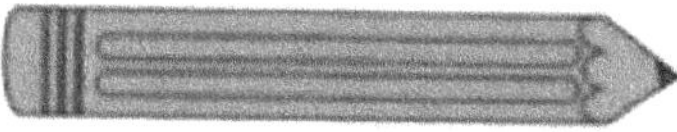

червен

color the word and
the picture in pink

red

Apples are red.

bleu

син

The night sky is blue.

percer

пробивна машина

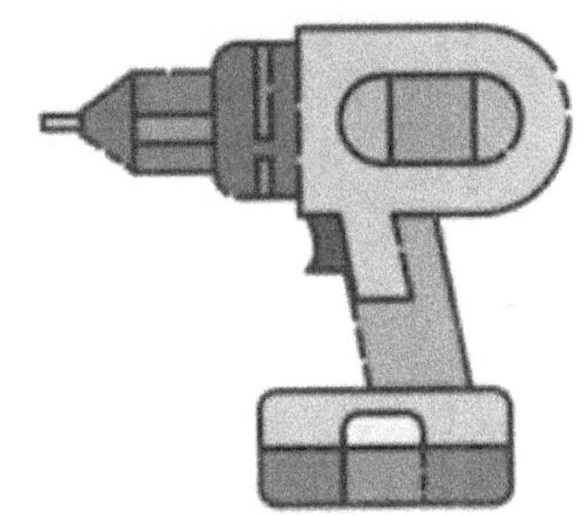

The drill will help us fix this.

marteau

чук

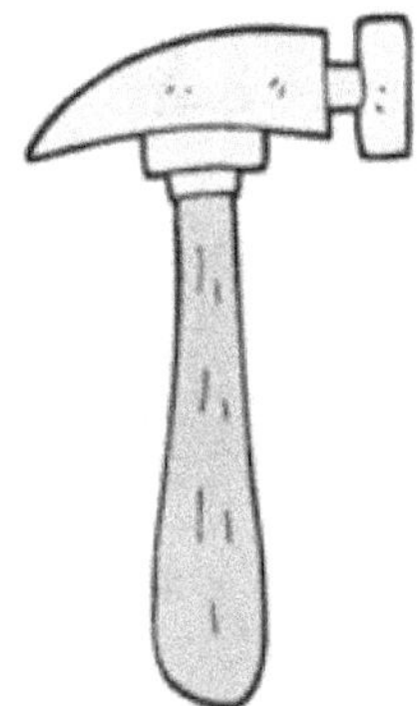

The hammer is going to nail the picture.

couteau

нож

The knife is sharp.

pinces

клещи

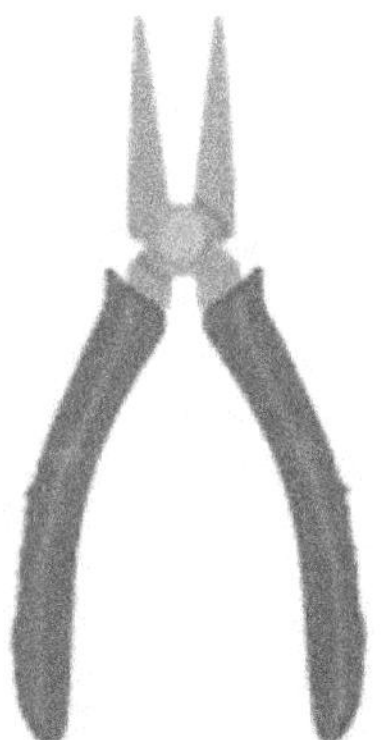

The plier is used for many things.

vu

трион

The saw can chop wood.

les ciseaux

ножици

I use scissors to cut paper.

tournevis

отвертка

The screwdriver can screw in the knots.

clé

гаечен ключ

The wrench can help unscrew the knots.

avion

самолет

The airplane is going to leave now.

vélo

велосипед

The bicycle is beautiful.

bateau

лодка

The boat is floating on the water.

autobus

автобус

The bus is going to school.

voiture

кола

The car is green.

hélicoptère

хеликоптер

The helicopter is looking for something.

cheval

кон

You can ride the horse.

jet

струя

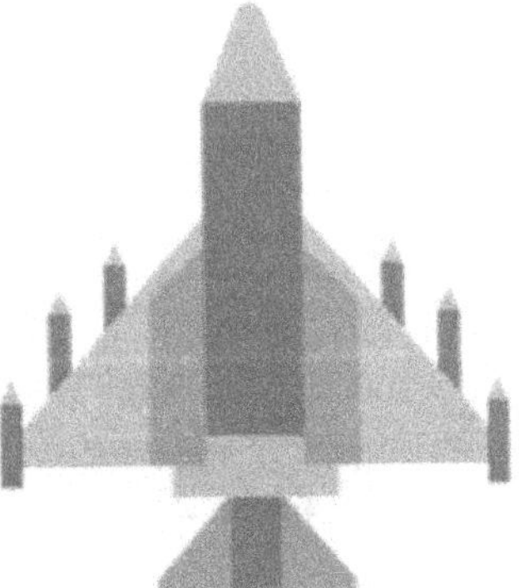

The jet is high-speed.

moto

мотоциклет

The motorcycle is on the road.

navire

корав

The ship is on the water.

métro

метро

My mom goes on the subway to work.

taxi

такси

The taxi has someone inside.

train

влак

The train is going slowly.

un camion

камион

The truck has stuff in it.

asperges

аспержи

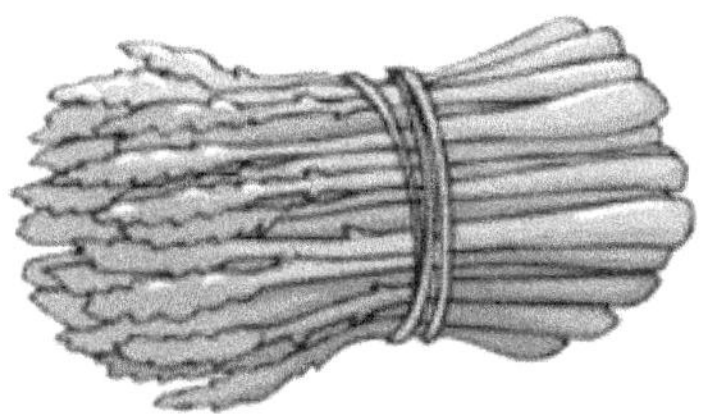

The asparagus is in a bundle.

des haricots

боб

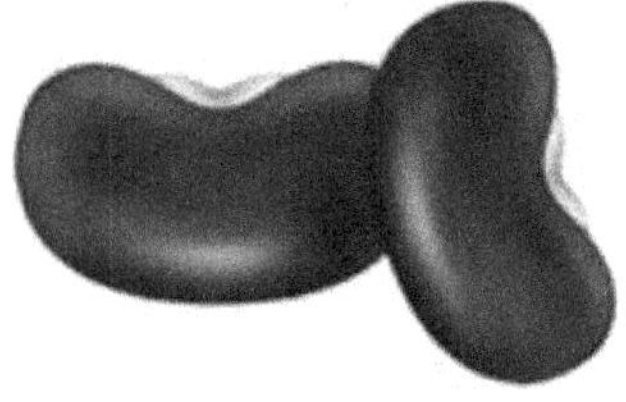

The beans are smooth.

brocoli

броколи

The broccoli is dancing.

chou

зеле

Bunnies like to eat cabbage.

carotte

морков

The carrots are very long.

céleri

целина

The celery has lots of leaves.

blé

царевица

Corn soup is delicious.

concombre

краставица

The cucumbers are cut into pieces.

aubergine

патладжан

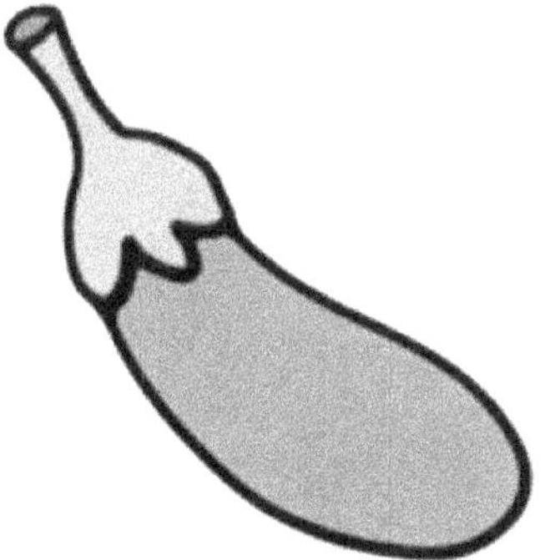

The eggplant is purple.

poivre vert

зелен пипер

The green pepper is juicy.

salade

маруля

The lettuce is all green.

oignon

лук

The onions make my eyes water.

pois

грах

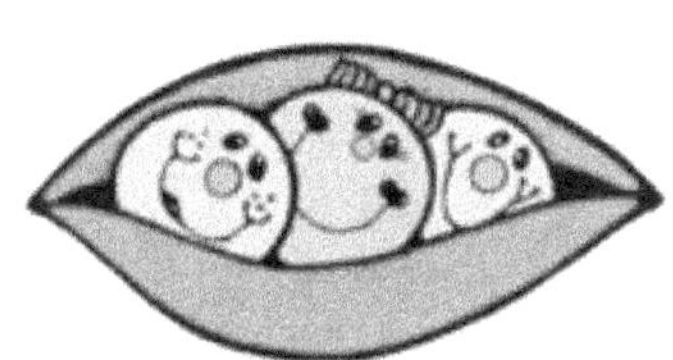

The peas are all in a pod.

patate

картоф

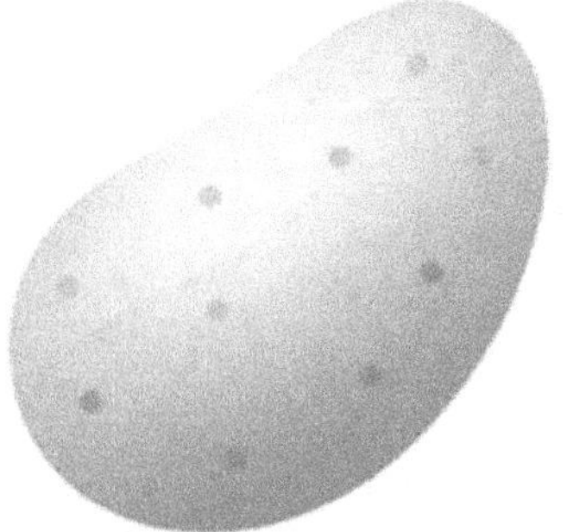

The potato is very shiny.

citrouille

тиква

The pumpkin is for Halloween.

un radis

репичка

The radish is a type of vegetable.

épinard

спанак

The spinach is good with cheese.

patate douce

сладък картоф

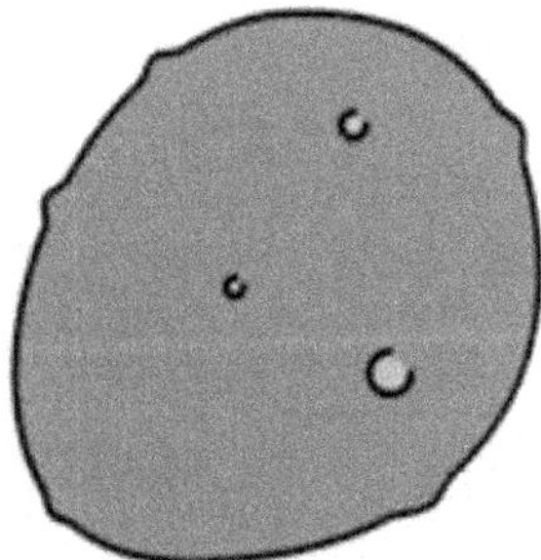

The sweet potato is quite sweet.

tomate

домат

I don't like to eat tomatoes.

navet

ряпа

My mom bought some turnips.

nuageux

мътен

The weather is cloudy today.

du froid

студ

I like cold weather.

cool

готино

The temperature is cold today.

brumeux

мъгливо

The fog is so strong I can't see the city.

chaud

горещ

The fire is burning hot.

humide

влажен

It's so humid and wet today.

pluvieux

дъждовен

It's raining very hard.

neigeux

снежно

Welcome to snow land!

orageux

бурен

I hate the stormy weather.

ensoleillé

слънчево

The sun is shining!

chaud

топло

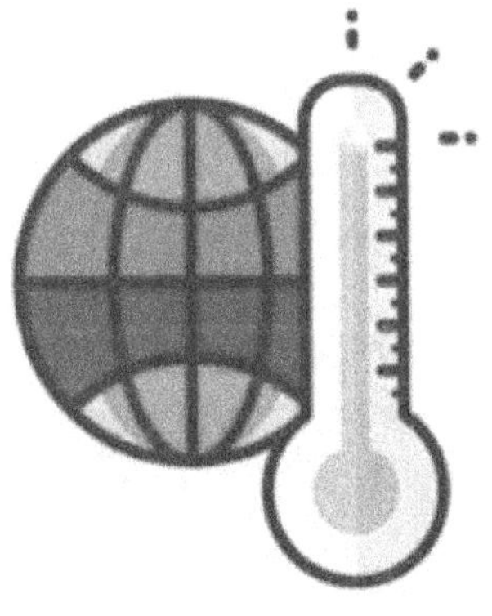

The whole world is warm today!

venteux

ветровит

The leaves are blowing away since it's so windy!

tante

леля

My aunt is very nice to me.

frère

брат

My brother is very fun to play with.

cousin

братовчед

I love going to the playground with my cousin.

fille

дъщеря

I like to read books with my daughter.

père

баща

My father is playing with me.

petite fille

внучка

My granddaughter has blond hair.

grand-mère

баба

My grandmother is very old and has glasses.

petit fils

внук

My grandson and I are very excited today!

mère

майка

My mother likes to pick me up.

neveu

племенник

My father's nephew is my cousin.

nièce

племенница

My niece is very good at playing ball.

sœur

сестра

My sister is so pretty!

fils

син

My son likes to play with toy cars.

belle fille

доведена дъщеря

My stepdaughter likes the color orange.

belle-mère

мащеха

My stepmother is pretty.

beau-fils

доведен син

This is my stepson, Greg.

oncle

чичо

My uncle tells lots of funny jokes.

bol

купа

The bowl has nothing inside.

tasse

чаша

My mom drinks her coffee out of a cup.

plat

чиния

That dish has a bone inside.

fourchette

вилица

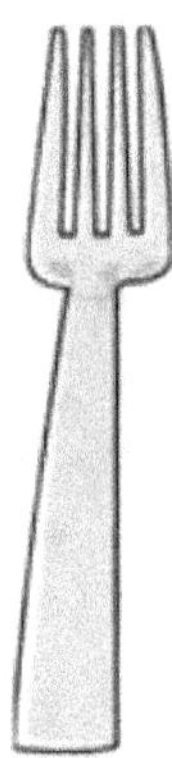

We have more spoons than forks.

verre

стъкло

I have a glass of water on my desk.

couteau

нож

I have a knife in my kitchen.

agresser

халба

This mug of coffee is for my dad.

serviette de table

салфетка

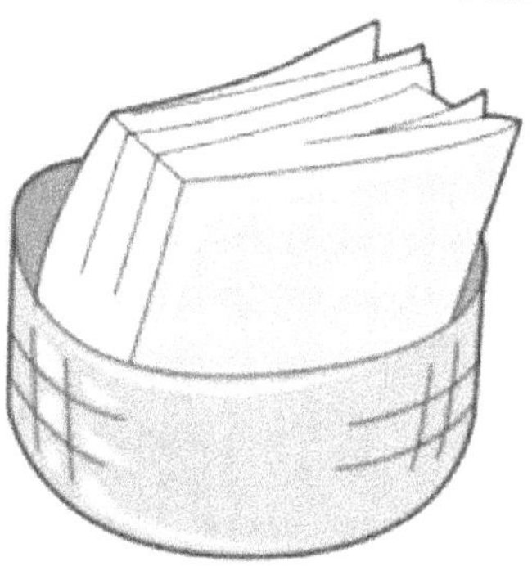

You can use the napkins to clean your hands.

poivre

пипер

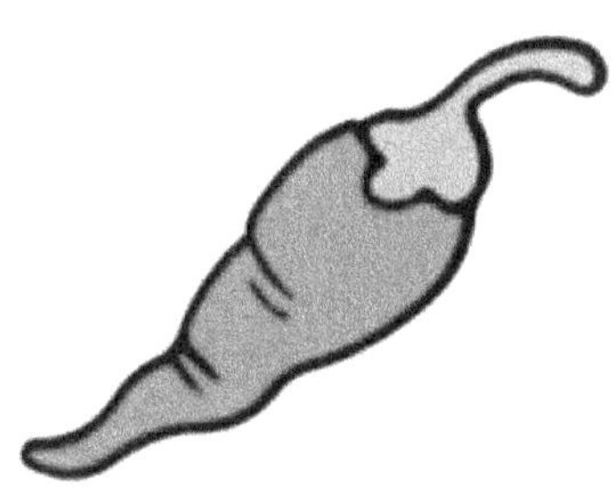

The pepper is very spicy.

lanceur

стомна

Pour yourself some lemonade from the pitcher.

assiette

плоча

Can you help me wash the plates?

salade

салата

The salad is very healthy for you.

sel

сол

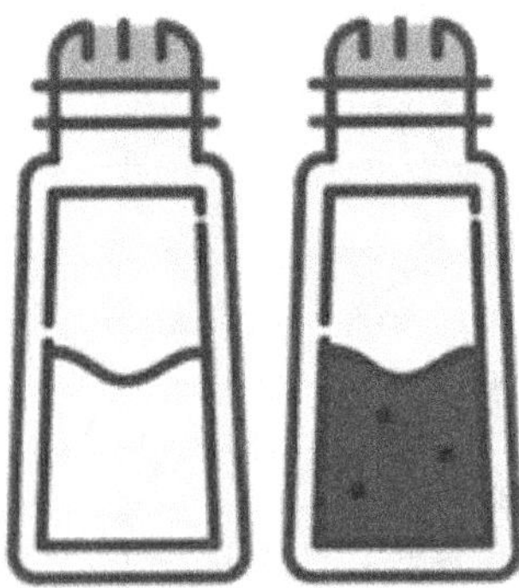

The salt tastes good with a few pinches of pepper.

soucoupe

чинийка

The plate is for my cup.

cuillère

лъжица

I use a spoon to eat my rice.

sucre

захар

The pack of sugar is very heavy.

dimanche

неделя

Sunday

Sunday is the day to go to Church!

lundi

понеделник

Monday

Monday is the day to start school.

mardi

вторник

Tuesday

We will go to the shops on Tuesday.

mercredi

сряда

Wednesday

Wednesday is hard to spell!

jeudi

четвъртък

Thursday

Thursday is the fourth day of the week!

vendredi

петък

Friday

My birthday is on Friday!

samedi

събота

Saturday

Saturday is the weekend!

cuire

пека

The chef will bake a cake.

ébullition

кипене

I will boil the eggs.

griller

печено месо на скара

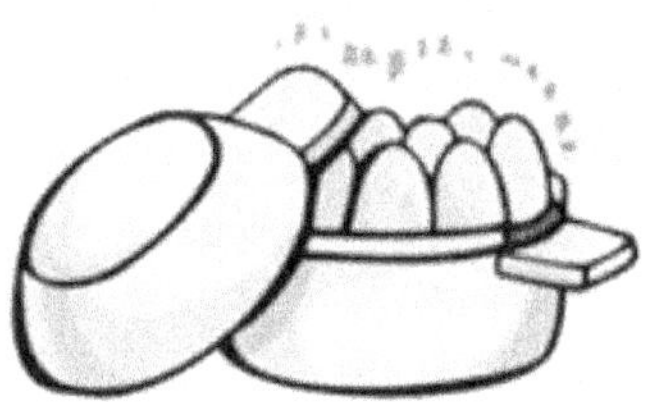

Broil is very yummy.

ouvre-boîte

отварачка за консерви

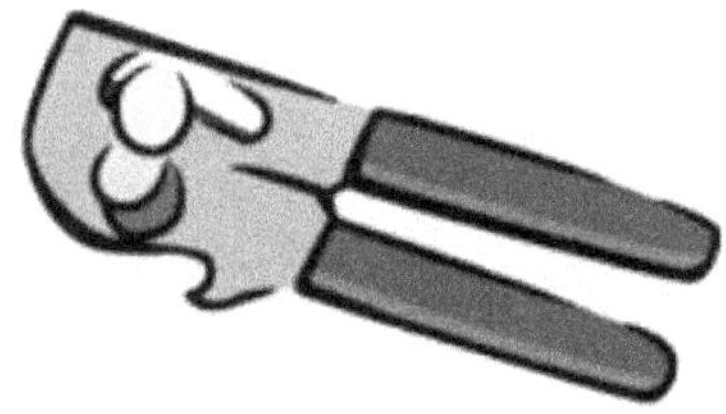

That can opener is used for
opening cans.

frire

дребна риба

The pan can fry lots of things.

gril

грил

We have a grill in our backyard.

tasse à mesurer

мерителна чаша

My mom uses the measuring cup
for baking.

cuillère à mesurer

мерителна лъжица

I use a measuring spoon to eat my dessert.

four micro onde

микровълнова печка

The microwave is used to heat food.

bol à mélanger

купа за смесване

She is using the mixing bowl to mix things.

serviettes en papier

хартиени кърпи

Dry your hands with paper towels.

poché aux œufs

яйце яма

The poach is put on noodles.

porte pot

поставка за тенджера

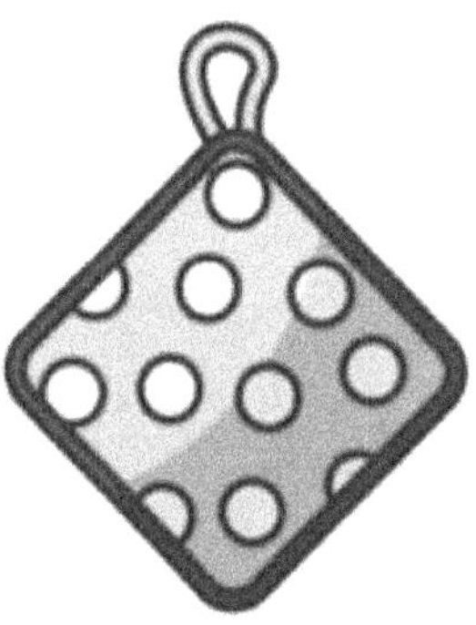

The potholder is soft.

rôti

печено

The chef made roast chicken.

rouleau à pâtisserie

точилка

He is holding a rolling pin.

brouiller

боричкане

My mom is making scrambled eggs for breakfast.

mijoter

едва се сдържам

The simmer is rice today.

couteau

нож

The knife is sharp.

cuillère

лъжица

I eat my food with a spoon and fork.

spatule

шпатула

The spatula will help us flip the steak over.

vapeur

пара

The steam is coming from the pot.

passoire

цедка

The strainer is used to strain stuff.

minuteur

часовник

I set my timer for 12:00.

fourchette

вилица

I have lots of metallic forks.

grille-pain

тостер

The toaster will toast my bread.

bouilloire

чайник

The kettle has tea inside.

réfrigérateur

хладилник

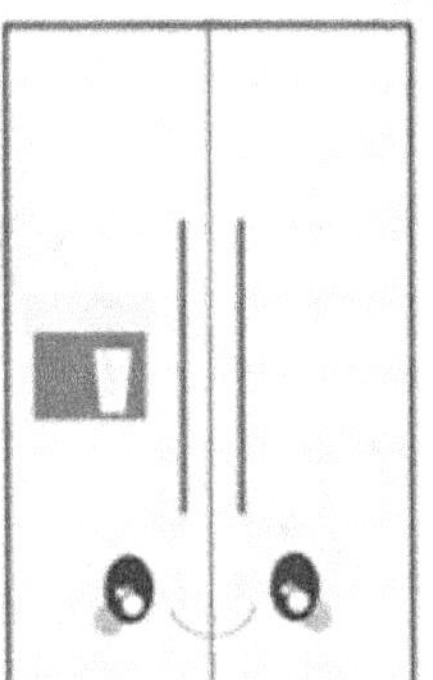

The refrigerator has lots of things inside.

mixeur

общителен човек

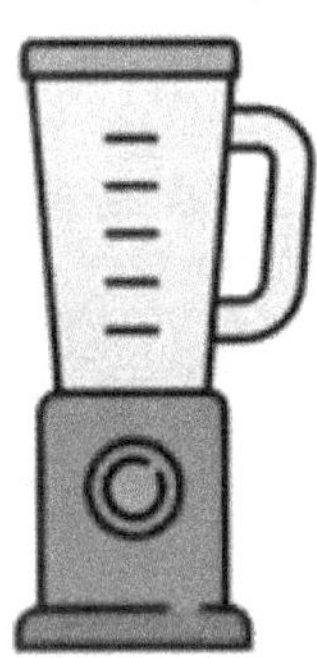

The blender will mix up my fruits.

cabinets

шкафове

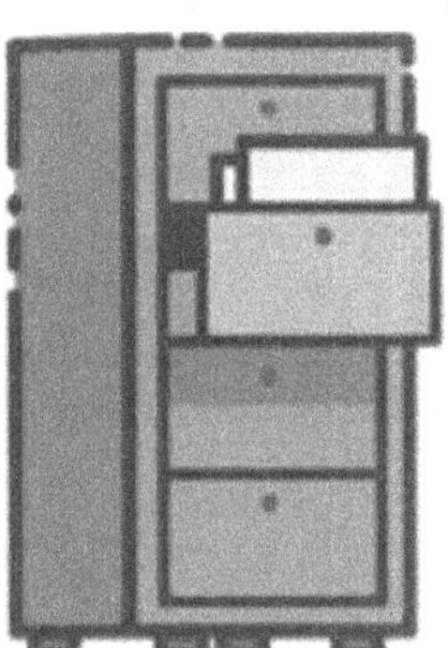

The cabinet has my paper inside.

placard

шкаф

The cupboard has lots of books.

four micro onde

микровълнова печка

The microwave will heat my food.

arrière

обратно

She has a slender back.

des joues

бузите

She kisses her mom on the cheek.

poitrine

гръден кош

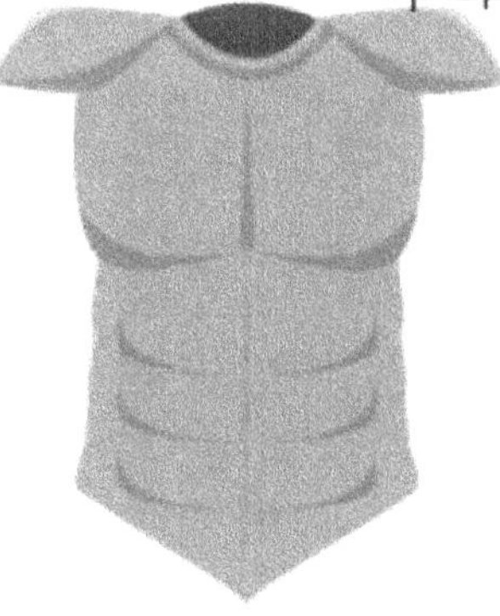

The armor is for your chest.

menton

брадичка

This is my chin!

oreilles

ушите

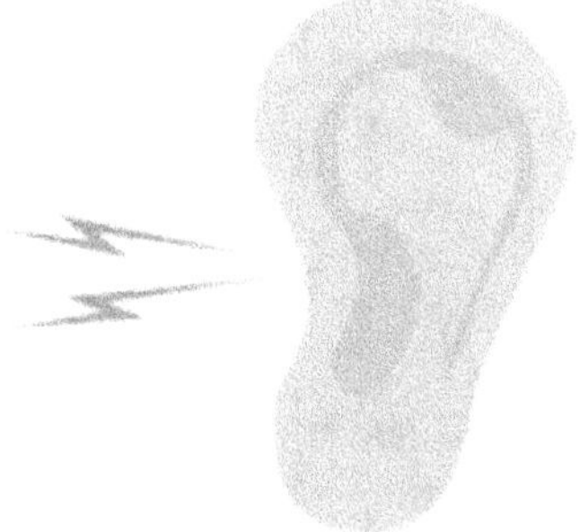

The ear is hearing something.

les sourcils

вежди

The eyebrows are raised.

yeux

очи

The eyes are blue.

pieds

крака

I have one pair of feet.

des doigts

пръстите

The fingers are waving at us.

pied

крак

My foot has five fingers.

front

чело

My brain is behind my forehead.

cheveux

коса

My hair is long and black.

mains

ръце

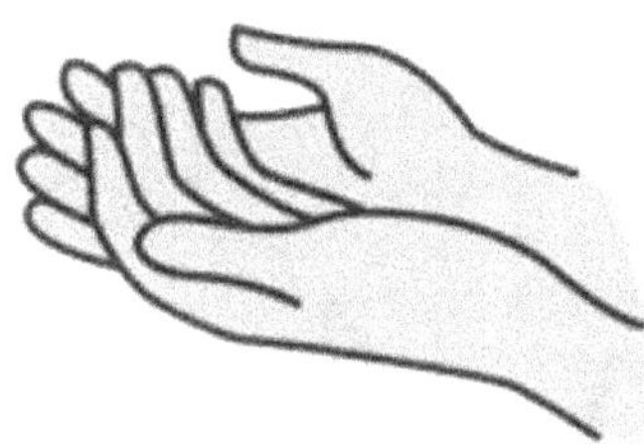

I will wash my hands in the sink.

tête

глава

She has a big head.

les hanches

бедрата

The gorilla has his hands on his hips.

les genoux

колене

She is begging on her knees.

jambes

крака

The tiger has strong legs.

lèvres

устни

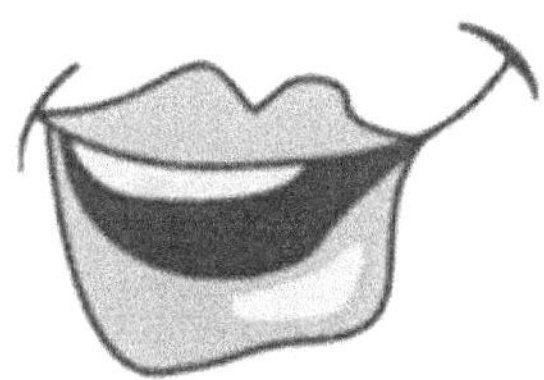

The lips have lipstick on.

bouche

уста

He is covering his mouth with his hand.

cou

врат

The necklace is very special to me.

nez

нос

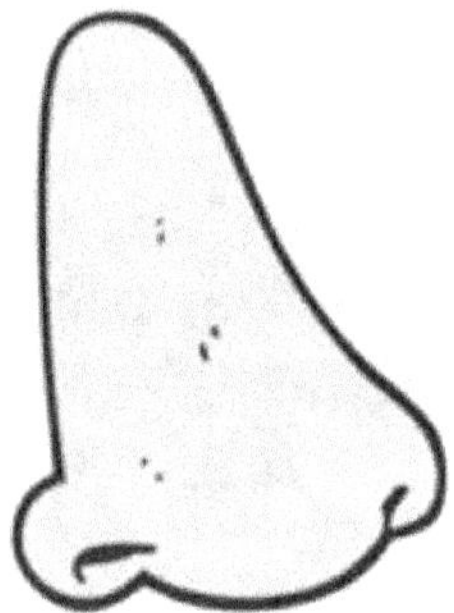

The nose smells something.

épaules

раменете

He puts his hands on his shoulders.

estomac

стомах

He has a big stomach.

les dents

зъби

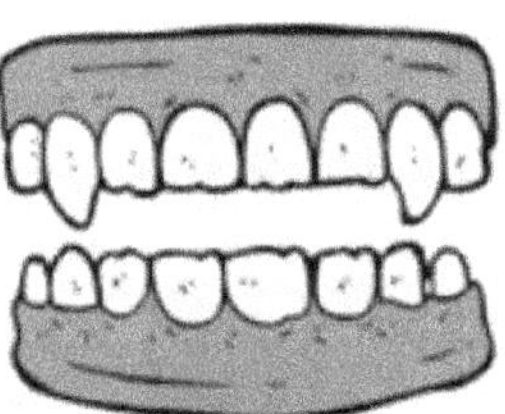

The teeth are clean and white.

gorge

гърло

He has a sore throat today.

les orteils

пръсти на краката

My toes are small.

langue

език

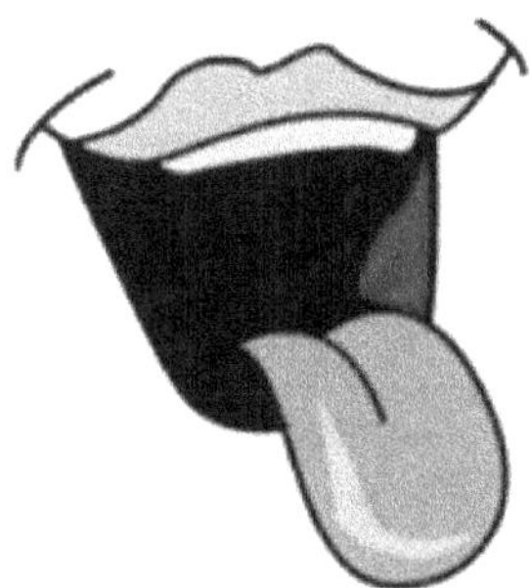

My tongue is licking ice cream.

dent

зъб

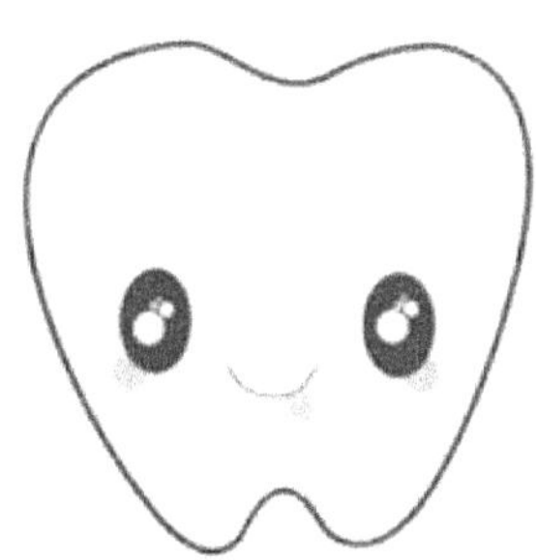

The tooth has big eyes.

taille

талия

He has his hands on his waist.

salopette

комбинезон

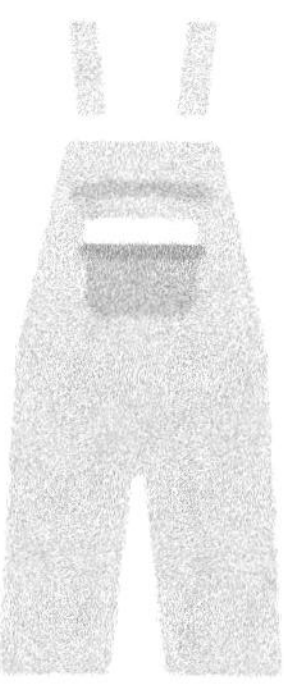

I bought these overalls for you!

mitaines

ръкавици

The mittens are very warm.

bonnet

beanie

The beanie is for winter.

tablier

престилка

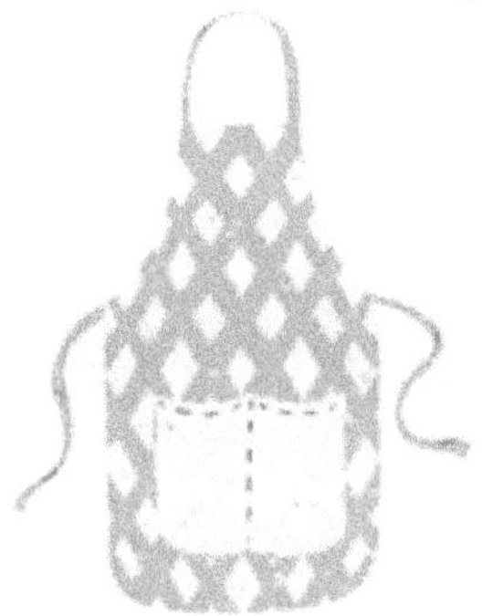

I wear my apron when I bake.

poupée

кукла

The doll is for my baby sister.

hochets

дрънкалки

The rattle is for the baby.

jouet

играчка

The toy is very fun.

couche

пелена

The baby has to wear a diaper.

berceau

плетена детска люлка

She is sleeping in her bassinet.

bavoir

нагръдник

My baby brother has to wear his
bib when he is eating.

octogone

осмоъгълник

The octagon is saying okay!

triangle

триъгълник

The triangle has three corners.

carré

квадрат

Square

The square has four sides.

cercle

кръг

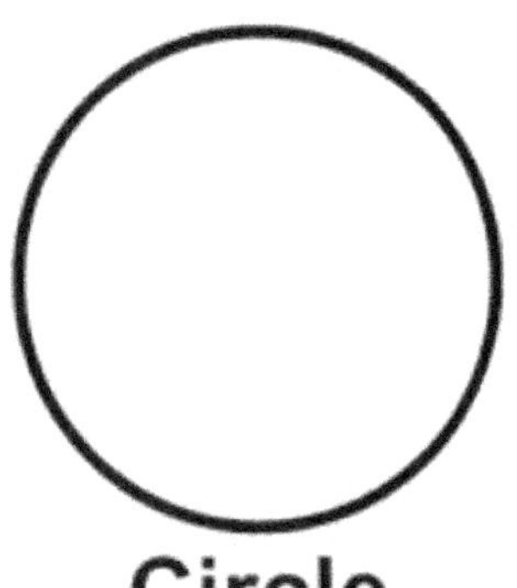

Circle

The circle is round.

ovale

овал

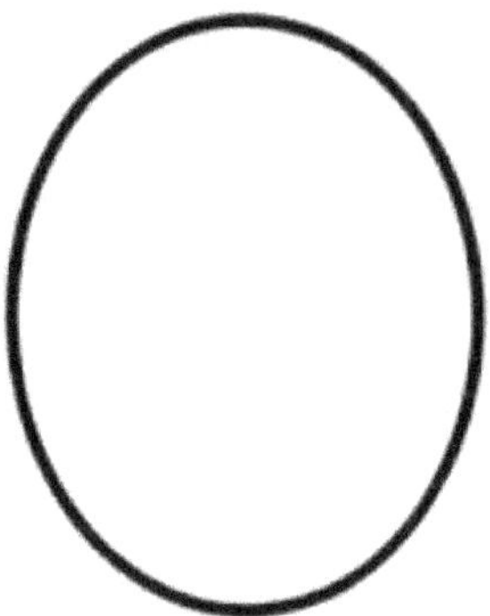

The oval shape looks like a circle.

cœur

сърце

I drew a heart on my paper.

traverser

крос

That sign is a cross.

la flèche

стрелка

The arrow is pointing this way.

cube

куб

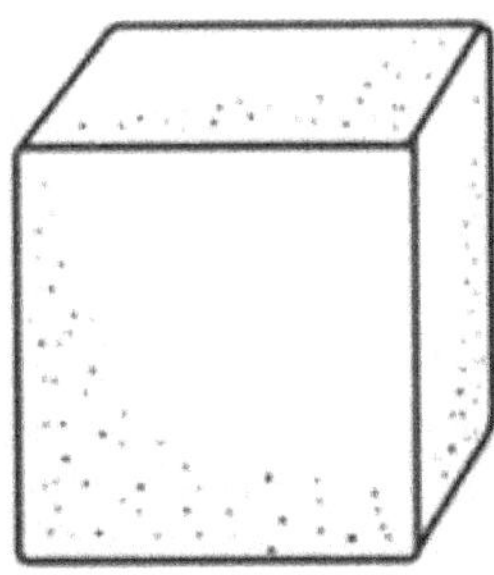

The cube is 3D.

étoile

звезда

The star is yellow and shiny.

tir à l'arc

стрелба с лък

The archery is where you aim.

badminton

бадминтон

My favorite sport is badminton.

criquet

крикет

I am very good at cricket.

bowling

боулинг

I got one pin down at bowling!

boxe

бокс

The boxing gloves are hot.

tennis

тенис

He can hit the ball in tennis.

faire de la planche a roulettes

скейтборд

He skateboards to school.

planche de surf

surfboarding

The shark loves surfing in the ocean.

le hockey

хокей

I like to play Ice hockey.

yoga

йога

He is closing his eyes and doing yoga.

épée

фехтовка

They are fencing and dueling together.

aptitude

фитнес

She will do some fitness in the pool.

gymnastique

гимнастика

He can do brilliant gymnastics.

karaté

карате

She is good at kicking in Karate.

volley-ball

волейбол

She is holding a volleyball.

musculation

вдигане на тежести

The girl with brown hair can do weightlifting.

basketball

баскетбол

He can balance the ball with one finger in basketball.

base-ball

бейзбол

The little chick is in the finales at baseball.

le rugby

ръгби

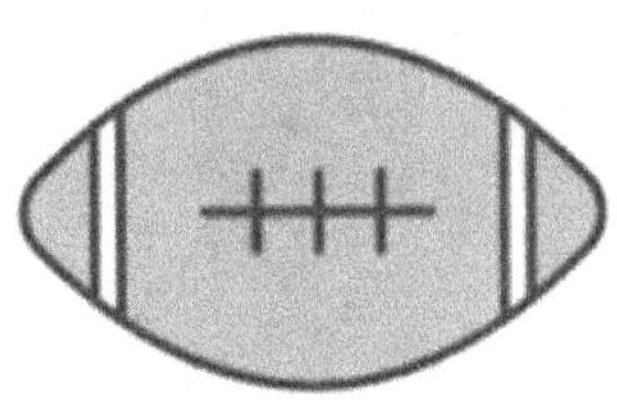

The rugby ball has white stripes.

lutte

борба

The sumo will compete in wrestling.

course de voitures

състезание с коли

He is number one for car racing.

cyclisme

колоездене

He is peacefully cycling on the road.

fonctionnement

работещи

He is running while listening to his earphones.

tennis de table

тенис на маса

My brother and dad will play table tennis.

pêche

риболов

He will go to the river to fish.

judo

джудо

She has a red belt in Judo.

escalade

изкачване

He will climb the ladder.

tournage

стрелба

He is shooting the archery board.

le golf

голф

She is going to compete in the golf competition.

balade

езда

He will ride his scooter.

asseyez-vous

седни

They are sitting down together.

se lever

стани

She likes to stand up.

bats toi

битка

They are fighting over the book.

rire

смях

He is laughing so hard!

lis

прочети

She read a picture book.

jouer

играй

He went to play on the slide.

ecoutez

слушам

He listened for the ice cream cart.

pleurer

вик

He cried because he got a bad grade.

pense

мисля

He thought that the test would be hard.

chanter

пей

He sang for the concert.

regarder la télévision

гледам телевизия

He watched TV the whole night.

danse

танц

She was a good dancer.

allumer

включи

The light is turned on.

éteindre

изключи

The light is turned off.

gagner

печеля

He won the contest.

mouche

летя

The parrot can fly.

couper

разрез

He was cutting his nails.

désinvolte

изхвърлям

He threw away the garbage.

dormir

сън

He slept soundly.

fermer

близо

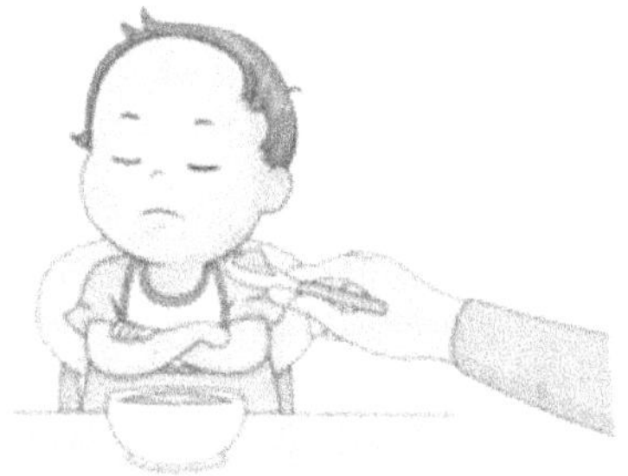

He closed his mouth shut.

ouvert

отворено

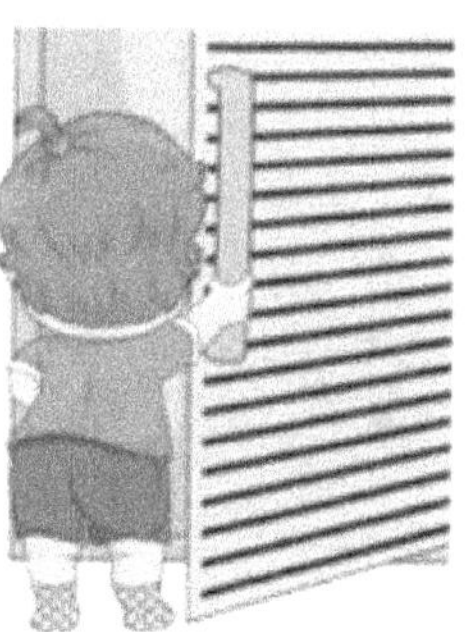

She opened the bathroom door.

écrire

напиши

She wrote with a pencil.

donner

давам

Santa gave her a present.

sauter

направо

She had fun jumping.

manger

яжте

The shark ate yummy ice cream.

boisson

питие

The old British man drank tea.

cuisinier

готвач

The microwave cooked his soup.

lavage

мия

You need to remember to wash your hands.

attendre

изчакайте

He was waiting for the bus.

montée

изкачвам се

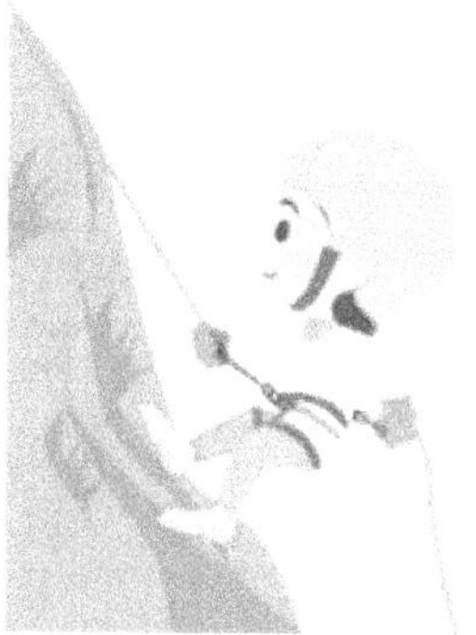

She climbed a lot of mountains.

parler

говоря

Two best friends were talking together.

crawl

пълзене

The baby crawled on the floor.

rêver

мечта

The Sloth dreamed about eating leaves.

creuser

разкопки

That strong man dug a swimming pool.

taper

ръкопляскане

The baby clapped her hands.

tricoter

плета

She knits with the purple string.

coudre

зашийте

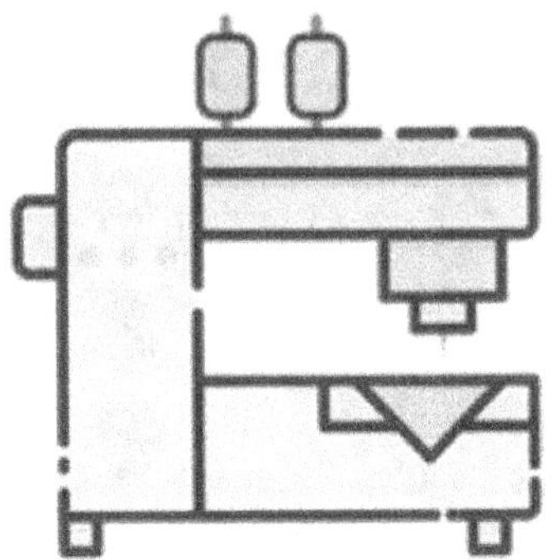

That is a sewing machine.

odeur

мирис

The perfume smelled great.

baiser

целувка

He kissed his mother.

étreinte

прегръдка

They hugged each other.

ronfler

хъркане

The tiger snored.

baigner

къпя

He took a bath.

s'incliner

поклони

He bowed to the judge.

peindre

боя

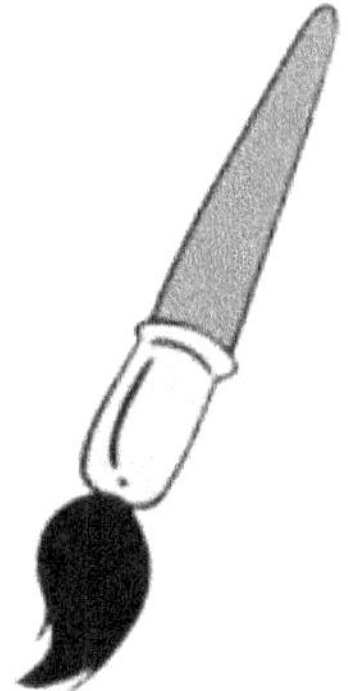

He painted a colorful picture.

se plonger

гмуркам се

He dove to the deepest part of the ocean.

ski

ски

The ski was expensive.

empiler

купчина

The books are stacked high.

acheter

купува

They bought cereal.

secouer

клатя

They shook hands together.

programmeur

програмист

He was a smart computer programmer.

vétérinaire

ветеринарен лекар

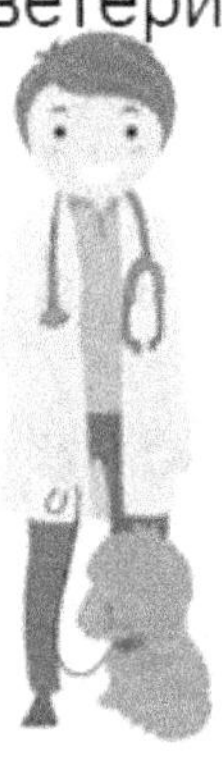

She is a veterinarian.

vendeur de rue

уличен продавач

That street vendor sells hot dogs.

mineur

миньор

That Miner will find gold.

prof

учител

The owl is the teacher.

groom

пиколо

That Bellboy is fat.

orateur

гов泳ител

The chicken is a great Speaker.

boucher

касапин

The Butcher sells fish.

pharmacien

фармацевт

That Pharmacist saved a person's life.

réceptionniste

рецепционист

He is a Receptionist.

politicien

политик

He wants to be a Politician.

guide touristique

екскурзовод

That Tour guide led us around Japan.

entrepreneur

предприемач

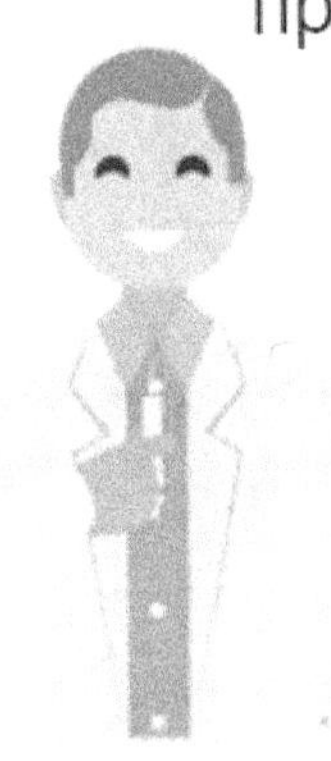

He is an Entrepreneur.

danseuse de ballet

балерина

She is training to be a Ballet dancer.

astronaute

астронавт

He is a great astronaut.

juge

съдия

That Judge is always fair.

avocat

адвокат

The lawyer is serious.

la caissière

касиер

She is a cashier at the market.

conducteur de taxi

таксиметров шофьор

He is a fast Taxi driver.

plombier

водопроводчик

That Plumber fixes toilets.

musicien

музикант

She wants to be a Musician like her teacher.

chef

главен готвач

The chef makes fast food.

boulanger

пекар

That baker is a bread.

artiste

художник

That Artist came from Italy.

acteur

актьор

That actor is famous.

barman

барман

The Bartender works in a bar.

coiffeur

фризьор

That girl is a Hairdresser.

évêques

епископите

He is a Bishop.

opticien

оптик

She went to an Optician.

fleuriste

цветар

She is a great Florist.

écrivain

писател

He is a famous author.

comptable

касиер счетоводител

My accountant is loyal.

du vin

вино

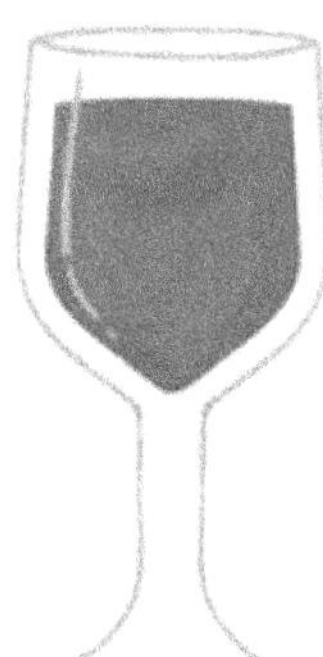

That wine tastes good.

café

кафе

That coffee is bitter.

limonade

лимонада

The lemonade is refreshing.

chocolat chaud

горещ шоколад

I drink hot chocolate every day.

milk-shake

млечен шейк

The milkshake has whipped cream.

eau

вода

The water is not cold.

thé

чай

The tea is hot.

lait

мляко

Milk is white.

bière

бира

The beer is foamy.

un soda

газирани напитки

The soda is fizzy.

smoothie

ласкател

The smoothie is a watermelon flavor.

milk-shake

млечен шейк

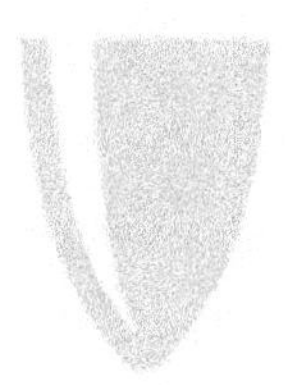

The milkshake has whipped cream.

lait de coco

кокосово мляко

The coconut milk is yummy.

du jus d'orange

портокалов сок

The orange juice is made from oranges.

cacao

какао

The cocoa is sweet.

fromage

сирене

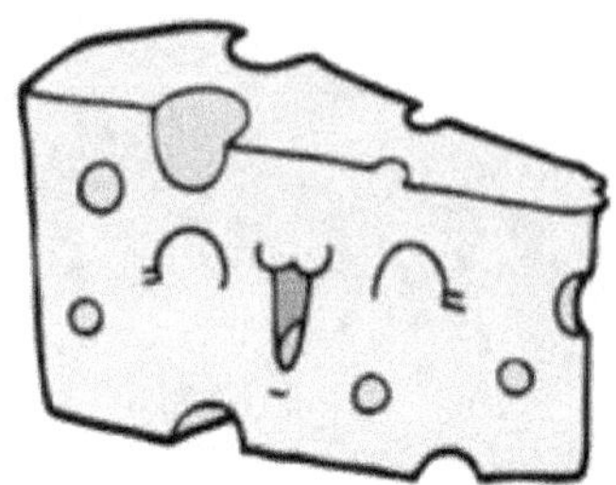

The cheese is creamy.

oeuf

яйце

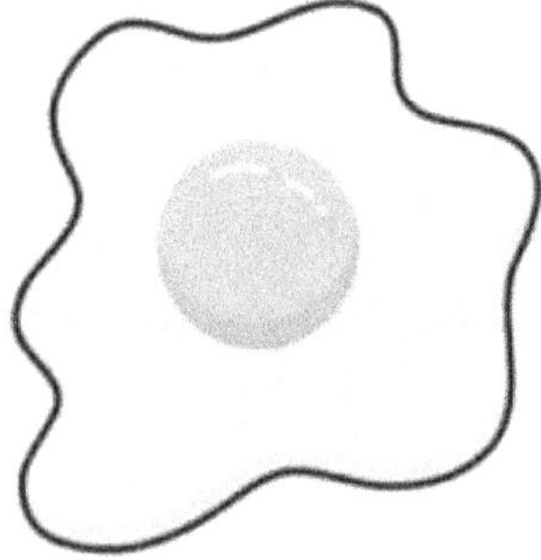

The egg is fried.

beurre

масло

The butter is put on bread.

margarine

маргарин

Margarine looks like butter.

yaourt

кисело мляко

That yogurt is popular.

cottage cheese

извара

The cottage cheese is put on crackers.

crème glacée

сладолед

They have a triple scoop ice cream.

crème

сметана

That is a lot of creams.

sandwich

сандвич

That sandwich is healthy.

saucisse

наденица

Americans love sausages.

hamburger

хамбургер

That hamburger looks happy.

hot-dog

хот дог

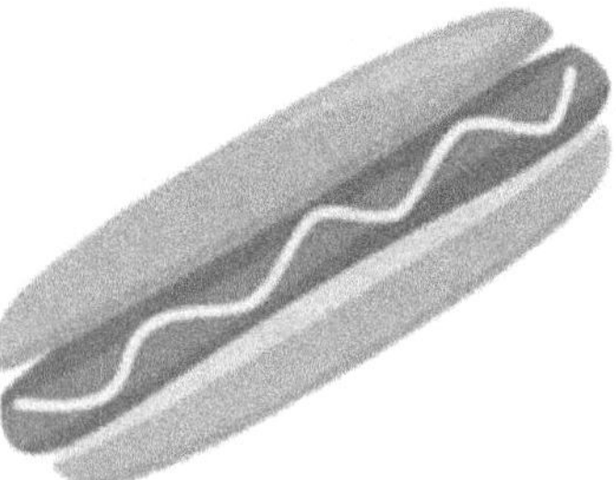

That hot dog has mustard on it.

pain

хляб

That bread is saying hello.

pizza

пица

That pizza is cheesy.

steak

пържола

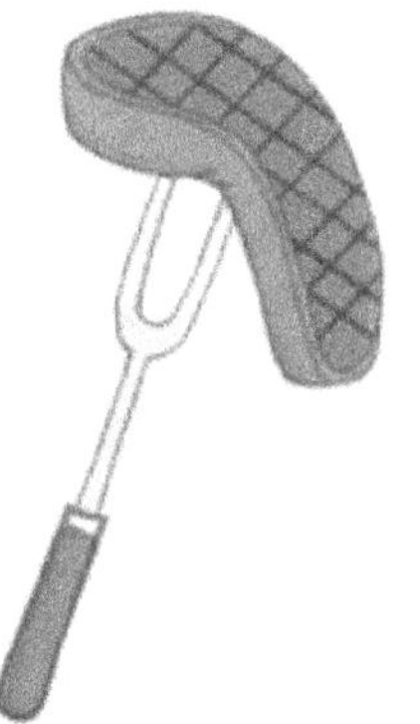

The steak was grilled.

poulet rôti

печено пиле

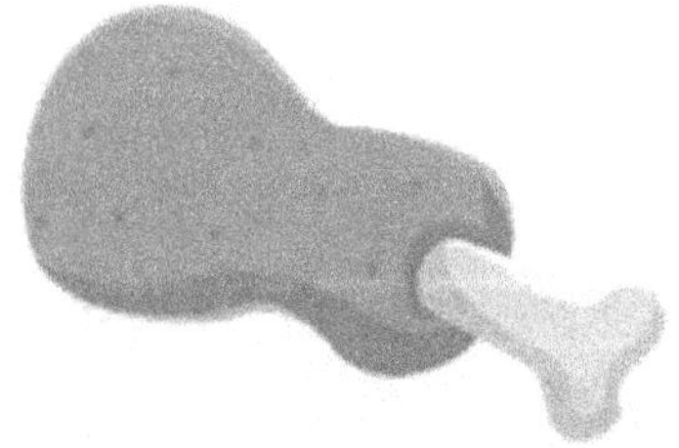

Roast Chicken is delicious.

poisson

риба

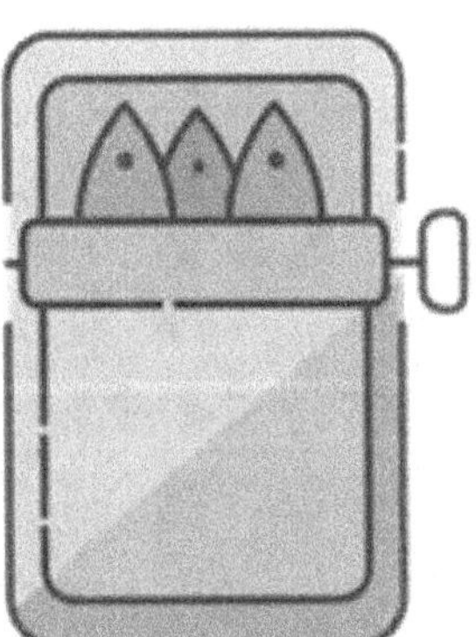

You can buy canned fish in the market.

fruit de mer

морска храна

Lobster is expensive seafood.

jambon

шунка

Ham can be put in sandwiches.

kebab

кебап

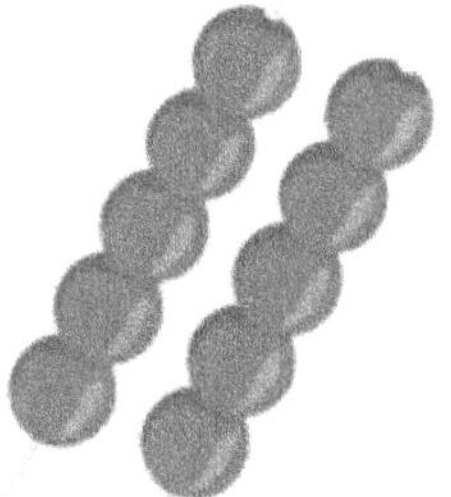

Kebab is a delicacy in America.

bacon

бекон

That bacon is smiling.

crème fraîche

сметана

You can dip your chips in sour cream.

vache

крава

Cows are black and white.

lapin

заек

That rabbit is fun to play with.

canard

патица

That duck is content.

crevette

скарида

The shrimp has six legs.

porc

прасе

That pig is pink and fat.

abeille

пчела

The bee has a stinger.

chèvre

коза

That goat has a white horn.

crabe

рак

The crab has two big pincers.

cerf

елен

That deer is sleeping.

dinde

турция

The turkey has a giant tail.

colombe

гълъб

That dove is carrying a plant.

mouton

овца

That sheep has fluffy wool.

poisson

риба

That fish has colorful fins.

poulet

пиле

That chicken is waking everybody up.

cheval

кон

The horse has a red mane.

chaise

председател

That wing chair is yellow.

meuble tv

стойка за телевизор

The TV stand can hold books.

canapé

диван

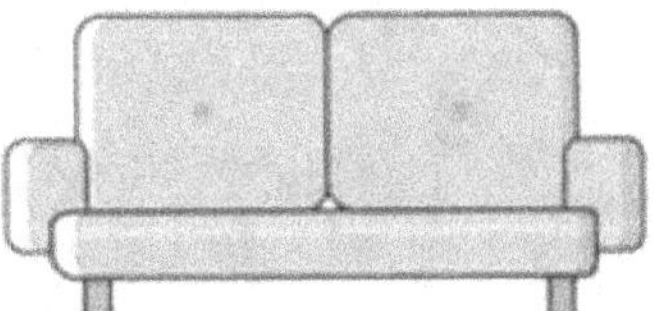

The sofa is comfortable to sit on.

coussins

възглавнички

The cushion helps soften your seat.

téléphone

телефон

The telephone is ringing.

télévision

телевизия

That television is big.

haut-parleurs

високоговорители

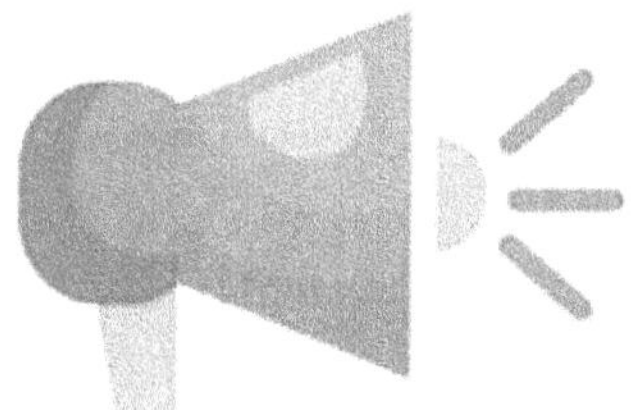

That speaker is used to increase the volume.

table d'appoint

помощна масичка

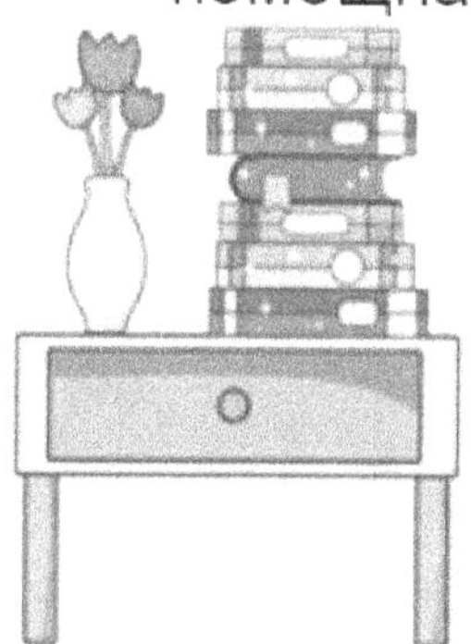

That end table is sparkling clean.

service à thé

чаен комплект

That tea set is from China.

cheminée

пожарна

The fireplace makes me warm.

télécommandes

дистанционните

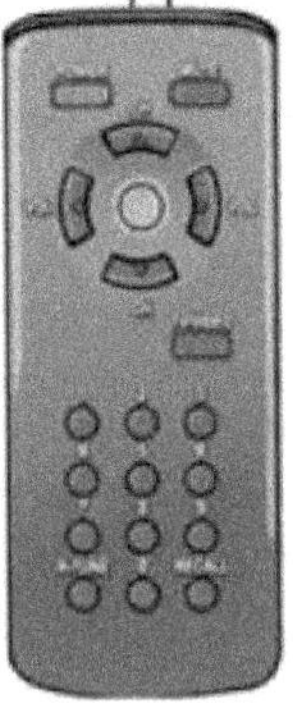

The remote has lots of buttons.

ventilateur électrique

електрически вентилатор

The fan is blowing wind.

lampadaire

подова лампа

The floor lamp is very tall.

tapis

килим

The carpet is soft and silky.

bureaux

бюра

The table is made of wood.

stores

щори

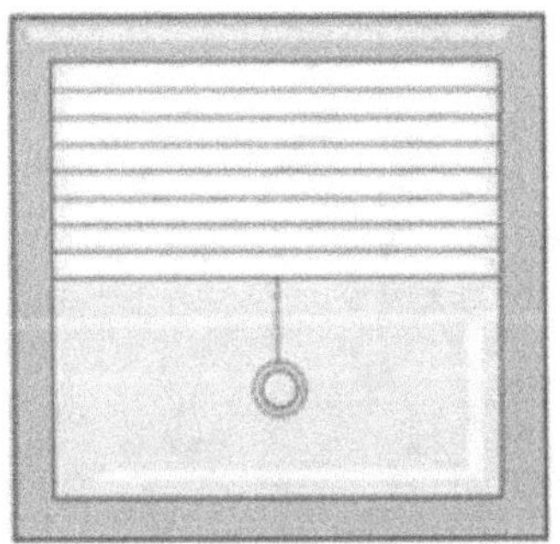

I will pull the blinds down.

rideaux

завеси

She opened the curtains.

image

снимка

The picture is about the mountains and the sky.

vase

ваза

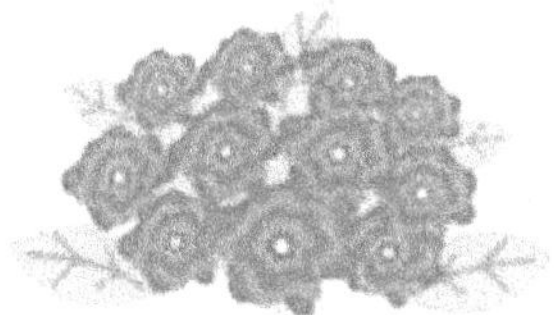

The roses are all in a vase.

l'horloge

часовник

The alarm clock is beeping.

oreiller

възглавница

The pillow is pink and yellow.

cintre

закачалка

The hat stand has only one hat on it.

mettre la table

тоалетна масичка

I have made up on my dressing table.

lampe de table

настолна лампа

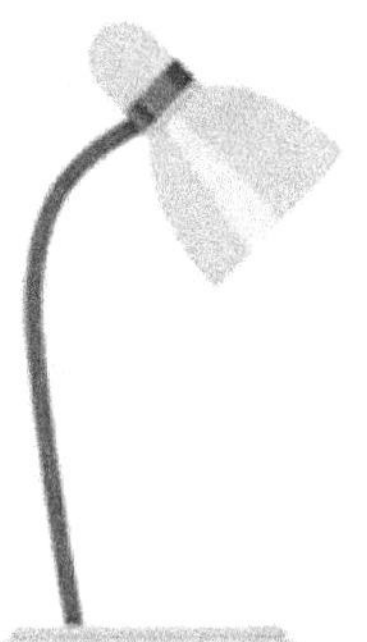

The table lamp will help me see in the dark.

miroir

огледало

The mirror is very tall.

planche a repasser

дъска за гладене

Don't touch the ironing board, it's hot!

boîte avec tiroir

кутия с чекмедже

You can keep your clothes in the hope chest.

table de chevet

нощно шкафче

The nightstand has my lamp on it.

lit

легло

The bed is charming.

climatisation

климатик

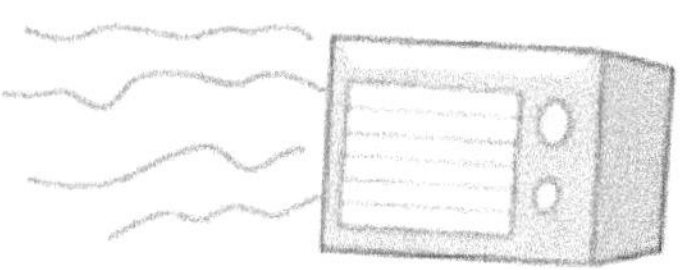

The air conditioner is cold.

cruche

кана

The measuring jug has nothing inside.

dentifrice

паста за зъби

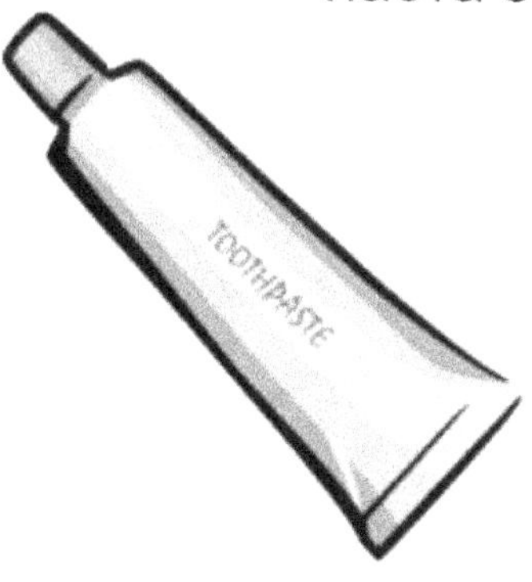

The toothpaste is mint flavored.

brosse à dents

четка за зъби

The toothbrush has toothpaste on it.

savon

сапун

The soap is very bubbly.

pince à linge

щипка за пране

The clothespin will clip my clothes.

cintre

закачалка

The hanger is hanging my boots.

sèche-cheveux

сешоар

The hairdryer will blow my hair.

shampooing

шампоан

The shampoo is used to clean your hair.

bulle

мехур

The bubbles are very fun to play in.

brosse

четка

She is brushing her hair with the brush.

papier toilette

тоалетна хартия

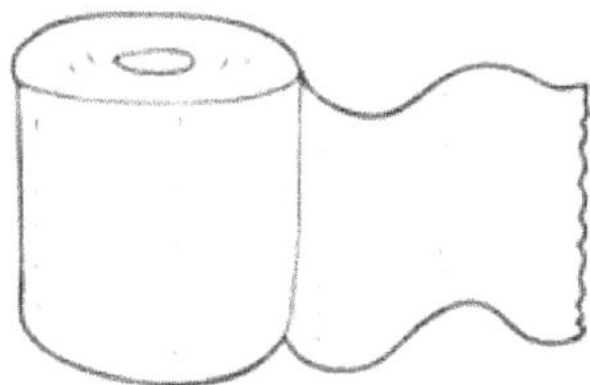

The toilet paper is used to dry your hands.

serviette

хавлиена кърпа

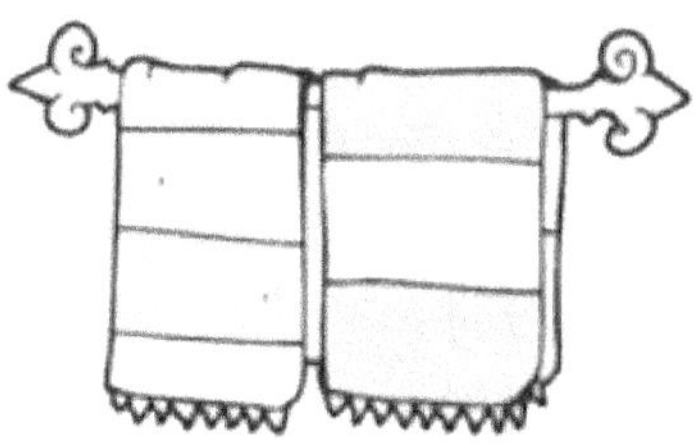

We have two towels on the rack.

corde à linge

за пране

My shirt is hanging on the clothesline.

douche

душ

The shower is spraying water.

baignoire

вана

The bathtub is comfortable.

lessive

прах за пране

The laundry detergent is used with the washing machine.

seau

кофа

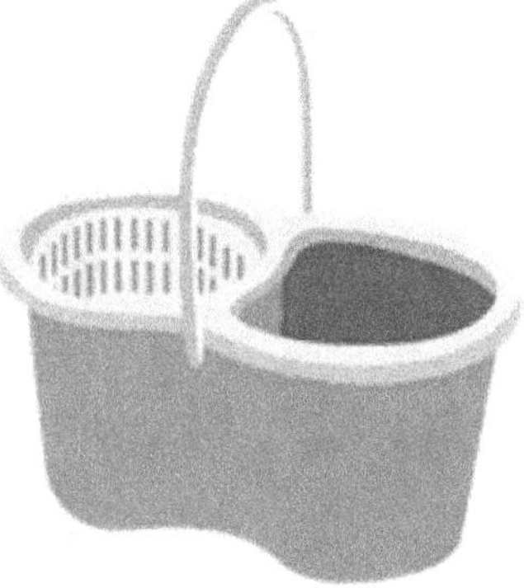

Can you help me fill up the bucket?

vadrouilles

мопс

The mop is used for mopping the floor.

savon liquide

течен сапун

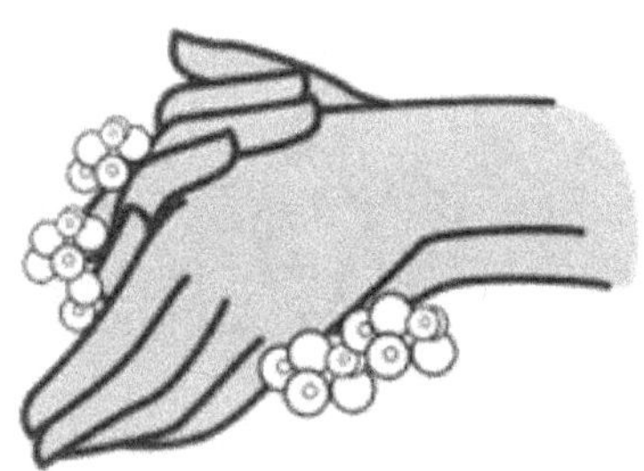

I use soapy water to wash my hands.

lessive en poudre

прах за пране

I will scoop up the washing powder.

sac poubelle

торба за боклук

The trash bag is full of trash.

poubelle

кошче за боклук

You have only to put recylcle trash in the trash can.

les puits

мивки

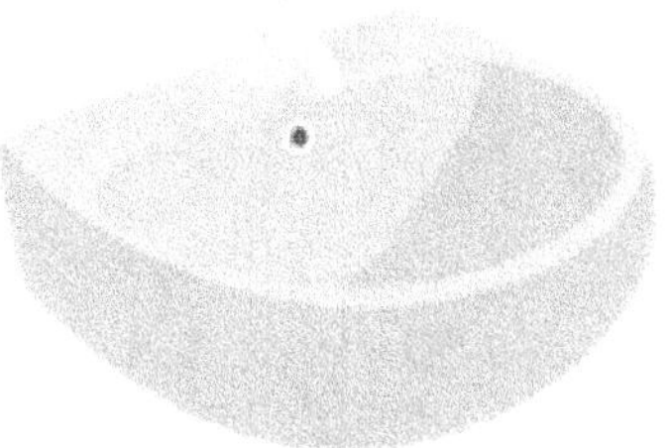

You should wash your hands in the sink.

cuvette des toilettes

тоалетна чиния

She let her bunny use the toilet.

machine à laver

пералня

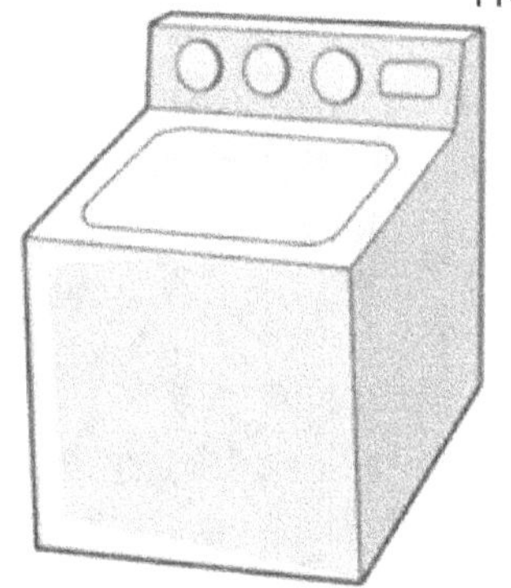

The washing machine wash your clothes.

panier à linge

панер за пране

She is putting all the clothes into the laundry basket.

le rasoir

бръснач

He uses the razor to shave his beard.

rasoir électrique

електрическа самобръсначка

The electric razor works faster than the normal one.

crème à raser

крем за бръснене

The shaving cream is fluffy.

bain de bouche

вода за уста

The mouthwash smells very lovely.

coton-tige

памучна пъпка

Q-tip can be used for many things.

brosse à cheveux

четка за коса

She brushes her hair with her hairbrush.

peigne

гребен

Her dad will comb her hair for her.

nettoyant

cleanser

Put the cap back on the cleanser bottle.

échelle

мащаб

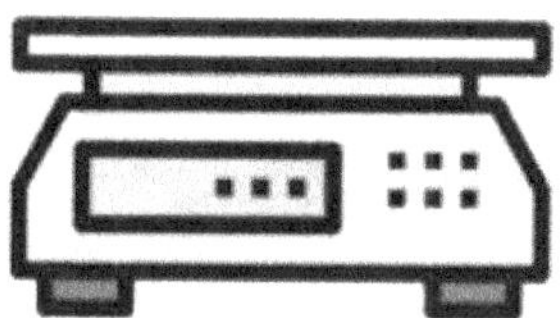

You can measure things on the scale.

papier de soie

носни кърпички

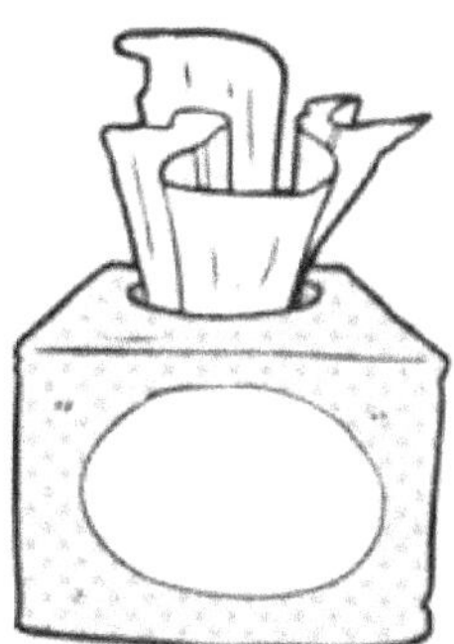

The tissue is on the counter.

jouets de bain

играчки за баня

The little duck is a bath toy.

robinet

кранче

The faucet is broken.

miroir

огледало

He is looking in the mirror.

tapis de bain

килим за баня

The bath mat is purple and yellow.